AF594848

WHERE. WE. WORK.

HOME OFFICES

Lannoo

INTRODUCTION.

THE FUTURE IS HYBRID

'I am so sorry, my camera is not working right now.' This was a lame excuse used by so many over the last few years. To be totally honest: my computer camera was never out of service. The main problem was the meeting décor, which changed from my bedroom wall to the bathroom mirror and the children's toys lying on the floor in the living room. There used to be a time when working from home sounded like a vacation. However, recently we learned the hard way that it can be quite a struggle. Designing environments that are both functional and inspiring was, is and will be an important challenge for interior designers and design lovers all over the world.

Steelcase, the leading manufacturer of office furniture in the United States, engaged 32,000 people in ten different countries in a survey on the future of work. Their research suggests that we can expect a much more flexible way of working. 'A Hybrid Future', as they call it, with splitting their time between the office and another location. That location can be a co-working space, a nice coffee bar or the privacy of your own home. The home office will become a permanent feature for many, challenging the aim to have a healthy work-life balance.

The way you organize your home office will have a huge influence on that work-life balance. That is why in this book we have created eighteen different chapters, to allow you to find the home office that suits you best. That's because there is no such thing as a one-size-fits-all layout to please all types of worker. After all, the Steelcase report shows five different types of home worker: the *Overworked Caretaker* is a person juggling work responsibilities and family needs, while the *Relieved Self-Preservationist* believes the home is the only place that offers psychological safety. Then there are also the *Frustrated Creative*

Networker thriving on face-to-face interactions, the *Autonomy Seeker*, who finds working from home more productive, and last but not least the *Isolated Zoomer*, who requires separation to maintain a healthy work-life balance.

Without any doubt, I am the first type, juggling to avoid catastrophe in both my professional and personal life. Therefore, the Kitchen Office is not my cup of tea. I would constantly feel the urge to wash the used teacup instead of meeting that important deadline. So, I have written this book for you from my Panoramic Office, with a slice of Library Office and some Gallery Office on the side. Many of the chapters can be intertwined: the Tiny Office can easily be a Hidden Office or a Playful one. And the Glamour Office benefits from a breathtaking panorama as well as from a well-filled library.

What makes the home office such a distinctive part of our private environment is the combination of technology and style. Plugs, chargers, headphones, screens, cables and printers: integrating those into an aesthetically pleasing space is quite a challenge. And then there are all the ergonomic requirements a home office has to meet: the height of your desk, the angle of your chair, the sitting, the standing, even the lying down. When you consider all these aspects, it makes you wonder how other people do it. And that is exactly where we step in. *Where We Work* is an inspirational book showcasing the most inventive, practical, beautiful and inspiring home offices around the world.
A warm welcome to this new permanent addition to our interior design. It is a tribute to a space we spend a lot of time in and an important option for all of you wondering how to integrate the home office into your house. And yes, we do realize that work is not the most important aspect of life. But working in an inspiring environment can definitely make your life easier. So, find yourself a good chair, brew some quality coffee and browse through the places where work and pleasure collide. Steal the good ideas, personalize the rooms, figure out what boosts your creativity, and above all: make it work.

An Bogaerts

TABLE. OF. CONTENTS.

Henry Moore
Paul van Ostaijen
MAX INGRAND
BAUHAUS
VERNER PANTON
FORNASETTI
MAGRITTE
VERANNEMAN
VASARELY
VASARELY
VASARELY
VASARELY

THE. LIBRARY. OFFICE.

WHO WORKS HERE?

- The most common Library Office worker is the lawyer. Lawyers tend to feel comfortable in the midst of their precious laws.
- Other professionals that blend in just perfectly are the writer, the publisher, the art director, the historian, the professor and the student.
- The Library Office is every minimalist's worst nightmare. Clutter is not just tolerated, it is encouraged.
- Especially in old houses the Library Office flourishes. There's an artistic feeling associated with a large book collection, a feeling that thrives in the surroundings of histori architecture.
- A Library Office is an ideal for any freelance worker wanting to make an intelligent impression on possible clients.

Let's pretend for a moment there is no such thing as Google, or the entire internet for that matter. In that case, a large collection of books is essential to get your work done. Look up difficult words, find inspiration in images and search for an aspirational quote that gets you through another working day. But even with Google at your fingertips, the Library Office has a lot of benefits. First and foremost it is a setting that doesn't require a clean desk policy. Quite the contrary. The more books surround your working spot, the more stuff is allowed to linger on it. Nonchalance is key. And it looks very arty as well. Combine your Library Office with some cool souvenirs, some great artwork, plants and the occasional sketch. Even when you are not creative in your day-to-day job, pretend to be an artist here, a writer, a highly acclaimed professor. Never underestimate the power of real books. They bring character to a room, decoration, history and life. In the Library Office you never feel lonely surrounded by all those stories. That's right: books can function as colleagues, with the major advantage that books always shut up when you are trying to get some work done.

THE.LIBRARY.OFFICE.

THE.LIBRARY.OFFICE.

⌃

It all starts with a few interesting books and before you know it the bookcase is flooding with them. Don't hesitate to stack books in different directions on that bookstand. And when it is really full, just let the library evolve organically throughout the rest of the office. Books on the windowsill, books on the desk and even books under the desk.

»

Some workers don't own a large bookcase to showcase their exquisite taste in books, or they lack the big wall to fit in such a statement piece. No worries there. The Library Office can be accomplished by just creating little piles of books and magazines scattered around your desk. Just call it a 'low library'.

May You Live In Interesting Times
ART & TODAY
PROVOKE
PURPLE PARIS
WONDERPLANTS

THE.LIBRARY.OFFICE.

THE.LIBRARY.OFFICE.

THE.LIBRARY.OFFICE.

The library isn't just a functional way of arranging books, it can also serve as a room divider. For those working from home, privacy is essential. The bookcase can be a convenient way to accomplish that. And depending of the amount of privacy you require, you can either put only a few books in the bookcase or fill it to the brim.

CLAUDE MONET
PAUL GAUGUIN
EDGAR DEGAS
PAUL CÉZANNE
ÉDOUARD MANET
Giappone
DÜRER
Arte
Mitologia
Oxford Paravia

THE.LIBRARY.OFFICE.

HOW TO MAKE THE LIBRARY OFFICE WORK

1

— The first important decision you have to make when installing a Library Office is determining whether you want to see books while working or you would rather not. That psychological choice will point out where your office will be placed: either in front of the bookcase or facing it.

2

— If you like the cosy effect books can have on a room, feel free to scatter some piles of books around the room.

3

— For an impressive library effect: choose a bookcase that stretches from floor to ceiling.

4

— If you are more the minimalistic book lover: create some visual tranquillity by colour coding your book collection.

DON JUDD
5FEB-2MAR
CASTELLI
GALLERY

BoConcept
WORK.

THE. HEALTHY. OFFICE.

Sitting is the new smoking. It might sound highly exaggerated, but it is a fact: our sitting life is contributing to the development of all kinds of diseases. That is why it is crucial to look at home working as a chance to turn that seated attitude around. Anyone thinking about installing a private desk at home immediately concludes that there should definitely be a chair and a table. Why? Studies show that working at a standing desk boosts creativity and productivity. At the same time it will improve blood circulation, lower blood sugar levels and reduce the chance of developing back pain. Are you feeling back pain right now at the thought of standing the whole day long? Nobody's stating we should all be standing over eight hours a day; the best habit to implement in your daily life is regularly changing position while working. You can sit for a few hours and then turn to standing, and why wouldn't you walk around the block while you take that phone call or read some reports from your home trainer? In coming years, the Healthy Office will definitely gain popularity, since it enables you to combine two crucial activities: getting your work done and exercising. Both of them contribute to a peaceful state-of-mind. Mens sana in corpore sano.

WHO WORKS HERE?

- The ironic thing about Healthy Offices is that the first to implement such areas are self-conscious workers who usually are in a really good shape already. People used to exercise and sports.
- The obvious professions for the Healthy Office are medical workers, personal trainers, gym teachers and professional athletes.
- A lot of really important business people with stressful jobs are realizing the impact their working habits have on their health and are also incorporating exercise in their daily routine. So don't be surprised to find your boss doing some push-ups while memorizing his or her next speech.
- Workers with a history of medical or mental conditions will be the first to avoid a seated lifestyle.
- People working in a Healthy Office tend to be both intelligent (about investing in their future health) and a tiny bit vain (wanting to look great at any age).

THE.HEALTHY.OFFICE.

IIf you have a spare room in the house it can be strategically smart to combine a home office and a home fitness area in the same space.

Make sure the standing desk is the right height. Set your standing desk at about elbow height. This means your elbows should be in a 90 degree position from the floor. As a guide, the average 180 cm (5 foot 11 inch) person would have their desk about 111 cm (44 inches) high.

dwell

«

A good reminder for exercising is to put your tools within sight. Put some weights on your desk or put the crosstrainer right in front of your desk. Make the confrontation with working out inevitable.

⌄

If you are in doubt about standing the whole day long, choose an adjustable desk. During the day you can easily go from sitting to standing and back to sitting again.

1

— Another convenient way to switch between standing and sitting is to add a stool to your standing desk. But make sure you don't just sit on it the whole day.

2

— Modern home trainers encourage you to check emails while exercising. This is obviously a great way to add some training to your working routine.

3

— A subtle way to move about is to create the habit of walking round the house while doing phone another is to put the printer on another floor. These kinds of change make a big difference at the end of the day.

HOW TO MAKE THE HEALTHY OFFICE WORK

4

— Working healthy starts with choosing a really good office chair. Whether it is a low chair or a stool, do not economize on ergonomics.

THE. GALLERY. OFFICE.

WHO WORKS HERE?

- This is no office for minimalists, because it tends to involve having little knick-knacks scattered everywhere.
- The Gallery Office offers display space to all kinds of designers, photographers, casting directors, location hunters and product managers.
- The Gallery Office worker is without a doubt an emotional person, someone who makes use of little scraps of art and souvenirs to trigger his or her creative mind.
- There is a nostalgic feel to a lot of Gallery Offices. Being encircled by images, materials and artwork you like can evoke a very comforting feeling, like being accompanied by your best friends. It can give an important boost to your work pace.
- The Gallery Office is an ideal business card for extroverts as it immediately shows the kind of person they are. I am what I hang, or something like that. Looking at a wonderwall can tell you an awful lot about the person behind the desk. So pay close attention, both both to your own wall and to the ones of those you work with.

In case you have just started to frame old children's photos: the Gallery Office is no excuse to exhibit fragments of your personal life. That is something you do in a hallway, or a corridor. In your Gallery Office the wall is decorated with inspiring fandangles. It can be literally anything (except childhood photos): scraps of fabric, pages out of a magazine or artwork that shakes your emotions, that triggers your ideas. Consider your wall as one big moodboard. Either facing you or ornamenting the wall behind you, it is an ideal backdrop for Zoom meetings. It gives the Gallery Office an intellectual allure, making it ideal for those who receive professional visitors in their home office. And that is exactly why it is not done to surround yourself with diplomas, children's drawings or even worse: embarrassing fragments of your stag or night. Keep things as professional as possible, even in the privacy of your own home. The more your office looks and feels like a 'real' office, the more real work you will be able to get done.

«
The first important decision to make is whether you want your wonderwall facing you during work or rather acting as a backdrop for your office. If you have the tendency to dream away easily, the latter would be your wunderwall of choice.

»
As spontaneous and casual as a gallery may seem, it should always be well thought out. Select artworks, photographs and other scraps of inspiration you want to use and determine whether they match in colour and style.

Hans
Melissa
is perfect

THE.GALLERY.OFFICE.

Selachii. (Plagiostomi).
4,5: Scyllium.
Mustelus.

»

Once you have made a selection of what is to adorn your wall, determine the best layout on the floor before you start drilling holes.

If you just had a small panic attack at the thought of drilling holes: this can be avoided. There are other ways to fix things: magnets, all sorts of clipping devices, pins and even decorative tape.

KØBENHAVN
GENT
STAYING IN

HOW TO MAKE THE WUNDER-WALL OFFICE WORK

1

— Make sure you alternate between big and smaller frames or artefacts hanging on your wall; it will make it look more spontaneous.

2

— Try to contain all your frames in one single wall. When every wall of your home office becomes a wonderwall it will look really messy and quite outdated.

3

— An option is to create a wonder-corner, using both sides of one corner in your office. For this kind of wonderwall, symmetry is extremely important, so everything depends on a good layout.

4

— A Gallery Office is the ideal place to add some eye-catching plants. They reinforce the homely feeling that your wonderwall creates.

THE. INVENTIVE. OFFICE.

WHO WORKS HERE?

- Let's just state the obvious first: the inventive worker is... well...inventive. He or she has an open mind and can think outside the box.
- An important feature for the inventive worker is confidence. Constantly doubting whether installing a desk on your rooftop terrace was a good idea will only slow the working process.
- In terms of jobs the inventive worker is someone who is used to colouring outside the lines. An inventor (if that is an actual job description) ticks all the boxes, as does a mediator or counsellor who is always looking at things from a different perspective.
- Whether working from the bath, from a hammock or from an improvised desk the inventive worker doesn't mind work and private life blending together. Quite the contrary. Work and life are not restricted in the inventive worker's home.
- The owner of an Inventive Office has the enviable capability to live in the moment, not overthinking design decisions and not worrying about what will be the impact of such decisions in ten or twenty years time.

The time is now. As we are reinventing the home office with no real boundaries set just yet, there is a huge opportunity to totally reinvent the concept. Nobody is stating that a fully equipped desk should always be present when working from home, nor that a chair feels offended when you leave it at the dinner table. The only two requirements that are essential for enabling homework are the possibility of standing or sitting and having some kind of table to put your laptop on. And WiFi of course. Those are the absolute basics. All the rest are factors you can easily play with. Do you want to attach a desk to your fish tank because the fish make you feel at ease? Or would rather work from the bath all day long? There are no taboos in home offices, as long as things work for you. The tricky part with Inventive Offices is that they require some explanation in Zoom meetings and when your boss decides to drop by unexpectedly, but even then the Inventive Office is first and foremost a determined choice not to compromise when installing a workstation that feels right for you. And only you. As it may be the place where you spend most of your time anyway in no other room should you be so stubborn when creating a personal universe.

For those with spacious houses: nothing is holding you back from installing several Inventive Offices. Since this kind of office is not perceived as an actual office, nobody will notice if there is more than one in your home. And as we all know, a change of scenery triggers

Even when your office layout goes beyond all imagination, a simple cabinet for storage can work miracles. Be sure to include enough storage space so your extraordinary office is not hidden in clutter and paperwork.

LENS'ASS ARCHITECTS
PROPORTIO
The Great Naturalists
ORBIS TERRARUM
THIS IS MY HAPPY PLACE
Deep Storage
MODIGLIANI
UNIVERSE
CHRISTOPHER WOOL
Actief
UITGEVERIJ PELCKMANS

neufert

HOW TO MAKE THE INVENTIVE OFFICE WORK

1

— Before deciding where to install an office, stroll around the house and try to determine which room makes you feel comfortable and inspired.

2

— As inventive as you may be, please consider such essential factors as ergonomy and privacy. Working from your sofa may sound very appealing, but it will kill your back and your housemates will probably kill you.

3

— We are all programmed with the idea that a desk and a chair have four legs. Consider the option of hanging a tabletop or a seating arrangement.

4

— When your concept or idea is really crazy in terms of form and layout, don't go too far in adding vibrant colours. We wouldn't want your office to look like a circus attraction.

THE. GLAMOUR . OFFICE.

WHO WORKS HERE?

- It will not come as a surprise that the glamorous worker is not the most modest person ever. The Glamour Office is made to be seen and adored, by as many people as possible.
- The Glamour Office is often home to successful CEOs who hardly use their offices since they usually have to be at the company's headquarters.
- And then there are the glamorous workers who aim to become the CEO. They already own the office, just in case things move fast.
- Some very glamorous jobs are for those who wear suits: the celebrity of course, and the celebrity's manager, also members of the Royal Family and people working in very luxurious departments such as those selling jewellery, watches, cars and boats.
- Anyway, the glamorous workers enjoy inviting clients and colleagues to their modest little home offices.

Most people use their home office to actually get some work done at home, but it can also serve other purposes. The home office can act as a showpiece to impress or even intimidate possible clients. Your house may be an absolute mess, but when your office is big and shiny and adorned with the right pieces of art and literature, it reads as a sign that you have made it in life. It is often a trophy office where the focus is on luxurious appearance, as opposed to the actual workstation that is usually situated elsewhere. Do not underestimate the mental effect of 'working' in a Glamour Office. You have never felt more confident, and that feeling can lead to great things (as well as to some nasty personality traits, but let us assume the best here). The Glamour Office can be two things: the proof that you are professionally very successful and the proof that you aspire to be so, using the Glamour Office as a self-fulfilling prophecy. Whatever works for you of course.

«

The Glamour Office is big. As big as possible. And it has a very nice view, preferably a view of the city skyline.

⌃

Cabinets can have a shiny finish, and have some details in shades of copper or gold.

HISTORIA SZTUKI
MODERN ART

ART
50 PHOTO ICONS
London
MODA

Make a nice selection of books to show off in your library. Coffee table books can linger in the office, as if you have just finished reading about wildlife photography in Namibia.

«

Be sure to add some really expensive (or expensive looking) artwork. Inform yourself about it, just in case any of your many visitors wonders about it.

1

— The desk itself has to be really big and cannot be cluttered. The cleaner the desk, the bigger it will seem. Just put a nice lamp on there and some fancy pens. Nobody uses pens any more, but just do it.

2

— An extra glamorous effect can be obtained by using heavy velvet curtains and big leather office chairs. Plural, because your guests will have to be given the opportunity to sit down comfortably as well.

HOW TO MAKE THE GLAMOUR OFFICE WORK

3

— A good scent is really important in the Glamour Office. You can scent your office with candles, sprays or regularly added fresh flowers.

boho
wild heart

THE. NATURAL. OFFICE.

As unnatural as working at home may feel for a lot of us, the Natural Office might just be the long awaited feature to turn that feeling around. The word 'natural' means many things to a lot of different people: from sustainable overlogical to green. In all of those cases it is important to realize that working from home itself is a very sustainable action, avoiding having to commute to the office. The connection with nature though, whether it is through the integration of plants or working with recycled materials, will enhance the feeling of being at ease. Not only do plants purify the air in your office, they can also purify the air inside your head, if you know what I mean. Moreover, working with natural materials will reduce the toxic particles drifting through the inside air to begin with. The Natural Office takes a lot of work and creative thinking to set up and maintain, but is definitely one of the most futureproof layouts. Especially in urban settings, this kind of office can bring the sense of nature we all crave for inside our houses. It will also determine our lifestyles. The more we connect with nature the more ecological our way of life will become. Seeing is caring.

WHO WORKS HERE?

- Obviously the Nature Office is used by people who love outdoor life. A strong connection with nature is indispensable.
- Natural workers are used to thinking ahead. They solve problems now to avoid them in the future. Global warming is at the top of minds especially the belief that every single action can contribute to its solution.
- There is a strong overlap between the users of the Natural Office and those of the Healthy Office. They they both contribute to a mindful way of working balancing both physical and mental health.
- Typical professionals practising in the Natural Office include landscape architects and gardeners, sustainability managers and brand strategists for eco-friendly products.
- The Natural Office is not just a desk and a chair, it is a lifestyle. This office is only a small part of the whole sustainable world; this home worker is creating it for himself or herself.

«
When you choose a nice spot in the house for your Natural Office, make sure there is some natural light coming in. You will need it as a personal fuel but mainly you need it to keep your plants alive.

8

THE WAY WE LIVE
A History of Interior Design
GILBERT & GEORGE
THE COMPLETE PICTURES
GILBERT & GEORGE
REBECCA HORN
THE ROLLING STONES
MARGIELA
GIORGIO ARMANI
MEXICO
TRAVEL

»

Avoid using glues or paints with a strong synthetical base, check ingredients lists so you know what you are doing.

»

In order to create an office that looks natural: avoid using too many bright colours. Keep it simple and in case of any colour-doubt: choose green.

MERCI SIMONE

1

— A home office is only sustainable when it can be used for years and years to come. That is why involving a professional is always a good idea. Although your workstation can definitely be DIY, it doesn't have to look like a DIY project.

2

— Add plants. Many of them. Choose air-cleaning, mood-boosting varieties that are nearly impossible to kill, like Philodendron, Sansevieria and Dracaena.

3

— Bright LED-lights are not in place here. You might get one of those solar office lamps, fuelled by sunlight.

4

— Try to minimize the number of electronic devices here. It looks a bit ridiculous to create a sustainable office and then install three huge computers, two printers and some extra iPads. Less is definitely more when it comes to digital pollution.

HOW TO MAKE THE NATURAL OFFICE WORK

L

THE. HIDDEN. OFFICE.

WHO WORKS HERE?

- Often hidden workers are people wanting to create a healthy work-life balance. When they are not working, they don't want to be confronted with the image of a computer screen.
- In urban settings, where space is limited, the hidden office is a perfect way to optimize the available space.
- In terms of job types, the hidden worker is someone who doesn't require an actual office or for whom the hidden office is an extra workspace outside the main day-to-day office. Perhaps an architect just wanting to follow up projects in the evening, a personal trainer checking appointments or a teacher doing some marking.
- The hidden worker is modest and unpretentious. He or she doesn't care about impressing friends and family with a huge desk screaming, 'I am so terribly busy all the time.'
- Often the Hidden Office is not reserved for one particular family member. It is the office you use spontaneously, for homework, to answer emails or make a few online purchases.

Not everyone wants to be confronted with emails waiting to be answered, quotes waiting to be reviewed or, particularly, paperwork waiting to be sorted. Seeing your home office all day long can be quite stressful. That is why a lot of home workers choose to hide their office space. There are two main strategies that can be followed when hiding your office. You can either hide it through design or location. In the first case, you blend in your desk so discreetly that it becomes an elegant extension of your interior design. The second strategy involves literally hiding your office away in a place hardly anyone visits in the house: under the stairs, in a dark corner of the attic or tucked away in a garden shed. Combining both design and location, the wardrobe desk remains the most successful layout for a hidden workstation. Tucked away between books, children's toys and the hidden television, no visitor can spot where a fully equipped home office will magically appear. As with all objects 'hidden' in the house, make sure you don't forget where you put the small home office. There is nothing more annoying than having to search for your desk when there are deadlines to be met.

THE.HIDDEN.OFFICE.

⌃

You do not want to draw too much attention to your Hidden Office, so keep colour pallets muted. For a wardrobe desk it can be cool to choose a vibrant inside colour, one you can only see when at work.

»

A Hidden Office has the huge advantage of also hiding your cluttered desk. Make sure you don't let that clutter escalate. Before you know it, the Hidden Office becomes a hidden clutter room you will despise.

HOW TO MAKE THE HIDDEN OFFICE WORK

1
— Ideally, the Hidden Office is integrated in the early stages of your building or renovation plans. Afterwards, hiding an office becomes tricky.

2
— A Hidden Office can be the ultimate solution to making difficult spaces useful in your home.

3
— As easy as a wardrobe desk may seem, make sure to provide enough power points and cable storage.

4
— The Hidden Office is not the place to exhibit family photographs or nostalgic souvenirs. It is an extremely functional space, decorated as minimally as possible.

JACOB

MONACO
75
10/11 MAI
MILK
ASIE OCCIDENTALE
CARTE N°16
PAR
EDOUARD
MER NOIRE
AZERBAIDJAN
ANATOLIE
ANTI-TAURUS
TAURUS
L. Tuz
Lac Ourmia
I. de Chypre
MER
MÉDITERRANÉE
MÉSOPOTAMIE
Désert
de Syrie
Euphrate
Tigre
IRAK
Firat
LIBAN
Lac de Tibériade
Désert
EGYPTE
Libyque
Péninsule
du Sinaï
Désert
Arabique
MER
ROUGE
ARABIE
NEDJED
CARTE
PHYSIQUE
LIBRAIRIE HATIER 8, rue d'Assas, Paris

THE. PLAYFUL. OFFICE.

Work is serious business. Except when you are a comedian of course, or a clown. But generally speaking, a job is what enables you to afford some of the pleasures in life. So we concentrate, and we focus. But that doesn't mean that our work environment cannot be fun. While some prefer the calm and quiet of a minimal little beige desk, to others a dash of colour is much more inspiring. The impact of colour can be enormous. Blue is an intellectual colour that boosts efficiency, while yellow is more of an emotional shade, promoting creativity and confidence. Green brings balance in life and work, it is an easy colour for the eyes to adjust to and it represents nature, of course. As you might have worked out by now, choosing one or more colours for your workstation is not something to take lightly. Colour can be a way to define the boundaries of your home office. Especially when it is incorporated into another room – the bedroom, the kitchen or the living room – colour can accentuate the presence of a different function. The most important rule is to stay true to your own personality. Show me your home office, and I will tell you exactly who you are.

WHO WORKS HERE?

- Definitely a confident personality. Someone who knows that the absolute worst thing that can happen after painting a wall is that you will have to do it once again.
- Whoever deals with colour in his or her day-to-day job will be more likely to add color to the workspace as well. So all jobs in art, graphics, fashion or design flourish in this inspiring environment.
- Colour can also work as a counterweight for a profession that is less dependent on creativity. Financial experts or planning managers can get the craziest strategic ideas when surrounded by a dash of lavender.
- The playful worker is definitely someone who puts as much effort and care into his or her working station than into his or her entire home. The home office is not a mere functional space but can be considered as a creative part of the interior design.
- In a Playful Office there is absolutely no need for a clean desk policy. So the playful worker is someone who can stand some carelessness, someone who doesn't freak out over a handbag or a book lying around.

«

Adding color doesn't always mean painting walls. Something as simple as a bright cabinet can suddenly make a home office look very playful.

»

A Playful Office is not only defined by colour: try to work with some unusual shapes, some nice artwork, vibrant accessories or a motivational quote on the wall.

Oh.

A Playful Office needs light. It is not the kind of workstation to immerse in soft, ambient light. When your office is playful then be brave enough to show it. Make sure there is enough lighting surrounding your desk.

Playfulness can be a good excuse not to clean your desk every evening. Creativity needs loads of impulses, you see.

DESIGN/
Warum
das Schöne
wichtig ist
Alan Moore
TRAVEL
2020

Liczby

Colour is emotion. In the process of choosing the colours that will define your workspace, stay true to yourself. Make sure you know what colours make you happy and which make you nervous instead.

»
One can also achieve playfulness by using darker, more saturated colours. It gives your office a more intimate look and feel.

LES TENDANCES 2021

HOW TO MAKE THE PLAYFUL OFFICE WORK

1

— Creativity is the main trade of the playful worker, so show your creativity by making regular changes in the design of your workspace. Those can be as subtle as changing a shelf or a painting on the wall, but can result in a complete metamorphosis. Playfulness is a state of mind.

2

— 'Playful' is not a synonym for 'childish'. When using colours and experimental shapes, be sure to add some 'adult' decoration so that your office does not resemble the crafting heaven of a 6-year-old. Such decoration might be a work of art, a planner or a detail such as a huge computer screen.

3

— This kind of office demands good preparation. It is not easy to make bold choices and combinations, so this is not something that you decide on the go. Create moodboards, test colour combinations and always keep an eye on the bigger picture, which is of course your home.

HENDRICK'S
A Most Unusual Gin
MAPPLETHORPE Perfection in Form

THE. MESSY. OFFICE.

WHO WORKS HERE?

- Obviously, germaphobes will not feel comfortable being surrounded by yesterday's cup of coffee, last week's mail and last month's cleaning intentions.
- The stereotypical messy worker is the confused professor, the mathematical genius or literate whizz-kid who can't find a system for his or her day-to-day paperwork.
- Anyone dealing with samples thrives on the Messy Office layout, whether a fashion designer, a carpet seller, a woodworker, an architect or an interior designer. Samples are life to them.
- The messy worker often has a character that thrives in cosy environments and this kind of workstation is the complete opposite of the Zen Office.
- Very social people who love to be surrounded by friends follow the same principles in their offices, keeping their favourite books and documents close by where they can see them.

Marie Kondo who? As peaceful and relaxing as a tidy desk may seem, for some of us it only stirs up stress. Like a blank page staring up at you. A big nothing. That is exactly why we are seeing a comeback of the messy layout in contemporary houses. Magazines and books lying around, dead plants crying for some water, and even bills begging to be paid. This is the organized chaos of the relaxed workers who don't regard their desk as messy but rather as one where everything is clearly displayed and is easy to access. The Messy Office often implies a high dose of creativity and intelligence and people who have this type of office are considered to have rather chaotic minds as well as chaotic living spaces. Is this chapter providing an excuse for throwing all kinds of rubbish? Not really. Even the messiest desk in this book is well thought out. The nonchalance is orchestrated and the mess meticulously laid out, in order to create a style that feels both welcoming and cosy, without resembling a hoarder's house.

Surround yourself with objects, documents and books that make you comfortable and happy. Deal with the invoices and fines and put them away. That is not the kind of mess you want your visitors to see when they enter your home office.

For your walls and furniture: choose rather dark and creamy colours, which don't contrast too much with all the essential objects that are placed on and around your desk.
The difference between a Messy Office and a hoarder's office is the ability to move freely about the office. The moment your stuff obstructs free movement, it is time to tidy up.

TOMATO

Although this office needs objects just lying around, make sure to have enough storage to put everything away. Just in case you fancy enjoying a Zen moment from time to time.

HOW TO MAKE THE MESSY OFFICE WORK

1
— First of all: there are limits to how messy an office can be before becoming absolutely disgusting. Last week's breakfast still standing on your desk is not a mess, it is very distasteful.

2
— Aside from the mess, make sure you have enough open space on your desk for your laptop or a cup of coffee. Messy doesn't mean totally full.

3
— In most cases, mess comes naturally. If you have the right personality for owning a Messy Office, all you have to do is wait and see. It will happen.

4
— Try avoiding mirrored surfaces in the Messy Office, since they will only multiply the chaotic layout.

and
PROVOKE
INTUITION

MY NAME IS CHARLES SAATCHI AND I AM AN ARTOHOLIC
La Subversion des images
1
2
3
4
5

THE. VINTAGE. OFFICE.

Do the names of Charles and Ray Eames ring a bell? Are you a sucker for Arne Jacobsen chairs and do you crave little modernist cabinets? Then your way to go when installing a home office is definitely to go vintage. Nothing adds warmth and style as easily as beautiful vintage pieces. And nothing is as pleasing as strolling round flea markets hoping to discover a vintage treasure. Moreover we are realizing that vintage design isn't just an aesthetic choice but also the most sustainable option there is in the field of interior design. As the definition of vintage is rather strict – items should be at least 25 years old but not as old as antiques, which are usually more than 100 years old – we will be a little more lenient in this chapter. An office is such an important functional space that it is often a challenge to opt for a full vintage setting. Vintage is much more a feeling than an actual age. A lot of famous brands are currently re-editing their vintage classics into modern, more comfortable versions, which is good news for the Vintage Office. Because choosing classic design pieces should not be a way of compromising on working comfort.

WHO WORKS HERE?

- The Vintage Office worker definitely has a soft spot for interior design. He or she enjoys decorating and knows a thing or two about the great designers in recent history.
- Since vintage design has a nostalgic feel to it, the predominant style of Vintage Offices is rarely minimal. Vintage workers cherish decorations, souvenirs, artwork and photographs. Therefore there is a big overlap between owners of a Vintage Office and those categorized as Library Offices and Gallery Offices.
- We see a lot of Vintage Offices in the houses of architects, designers, historians, graphic designers and art dealers.
- Vintage workers tend to regularly change the layout of their office. When they discover another vintage treasure the whole room can be submitted to change in order to fit the new discovery in.
- Vintage lovers usually have an aesthetically trained eye. That means that these kinds of office are usually located in beautifully decorated houses and apartments.

LE MUSÉE D'ISRAËL
Sunflowers for Van Gogh

«

Installing a Vintage Office is not something you do over one night. It can take weeks, months or even years to find the perfect treasures.

»

Therefore, a Vintage Office is difficult to plan. It all depends on what you can find. It is easier to go shopping first and then decide about the layout of your office. Searching for a vintage desk of an exact width can be quite a crusade.

WALTER VAN BEIRENDONCK

»
When buying vintage for your office, pay close attention to the condition of the furniture and don't compromise on ergonomics. Be aware that about 70 years ago the average height of people was smaller than it now is.

«
Instead of buying vintage furniture you can opt for buying new versions of old classics. Especially if you regularly suffer from back pain or another form of discomfort, it may be a good idea to go for new and improved now. Thoroughly testing the things you find is a must.

THE.VINTAGE.OFFICE.

HOW TO MAKE THE VINTAGE OFFICE WORK

1

— Combining vintage with new design creates an interesting tension. It also prevents your office from looking old rather than vintage.

2

— A Vintage Office calls for interesting books (on vintage!), artwork, souvenirs and out-of-the-box decoration. A piece of taxidermy too maybe?

3

— Vintage desks and chairs are often made of wood. When you have a lot of wooden design in your office, be sure to balance that with an interesting colour on your walls. A contrasting colour such as red, green or black always works and it makes the vintage stand out even more.

4

— Don't just stroll, but scroll. Amusing as a visit to real flea markets and vintage shops can be, the largest offer of vintage furniture is to be found online.

SEURAT
ART DECO
BAUHAUS
DAVID BOWIE
VERANNEMAN
ONZE VISSERS
pirelli

BRYCE COURTENAY
The Story of DANNY DUNN
MINETTE WALTERS
THE ECHO
BRYCE COURTENAY
Jessica
DI MORRISSEY
SCATTER the STARS

THE. KITCHEN. OFFICE.

WHO WORKS HERE?

- The kitchen worker often has no other choice than to work in the kitchen. Microworkers not having the spare square metres in the living room or bedroom just have to figure out a way to work at the kitchen table.
- On the other hand, there are a lot of single workers opting for the Kitchen Office. When you are the only one in the house the kitchen is as good a place as any other.
- Of course, when your work is culinary oriëntated, when you are a chef, a brewer or a gastronomic product manager, working in a kitchen environment can be considered as totally normal.
- In all other cases the kitchen worker has to prepare for a serious challenge, especially around coffee break, lunch and snack time. 'Focus' is the kitchen worker's middle name.
- So for all those reasons: work and life blend together at kitchen level. There is no such thing as a work-life balance. Emails can still be checked while cutting carrots for the evening meal.

We have all worked there at some stage: The kitchen. It is both the easiest and the hardest office to realize. For many of us, the Kitchen Office is the very first home office, just a matter of a seat at the kitchen table and flipping that laptop open. It is also the place where many realize: 'I have had enough. I cannot keep on working here.' And they move. Organizing a successful Kitchen Office is quite a challenge, mainly because for many the kitchen is the heart of the home, where family members drop in every single hour of the day. It is the place where there is often someone cooking, eating or cleaning. Where coffees are made, water bottles are filled and small talk is cheap. To tackle all that, the Kitchen Office has to be well thought out and the kitchen worker has to develop an iron working mentality, resisting these influences like a pro. One big advantage: the coffee is only a few steps away.

THE.KITCHEN.OFFICE.

«
Try not to face the kitchen from your desk. Sit with your back to the kitchen to minimize interaction with other members of the family during your work.

»
To cut out as much noise as possible, a good headset can be a relief during kitchen rush hour. Set up some strict house rules with your fellow inhabitants, so that they don't disturb you every five minutes.

It is a good idea to install a separate desk in the kitchen that is not the table you eat on. It can be a burden to have always to put your stuff away when the table is set. And working next to a pile of dirty dishes is not the most inspiring setting.

THE.KITCHEN.OFFICE.

THE.KITCHEN.OFFICE.

1
— When there is no other option than to install your laptop at the kitchen table, make sure you have enough light to read and that you use a proper office chair, or at least one that is ergonomically OK. Your back will thank you for it.

2
— A scented candle can be a huge asset to your little Kitchen Office, clearing out all the culinary odours spreading around.

3
— A good extraction hood in the kitchen is well worth the investment when you consider using the room to work in.

4
— The Hidden Office is a good concept to adopt for the Kitchen Office. Try to hide your office in a cupboard when it is not being used.

HOW TO MAKE THE KITCHEN OFFICE WORK

THE. DUO. OFFICE.

WHO WORKS HERE?

- The power couple, of course: husband and wife, husband and husband, or wife and wife. Managing their own company, founded together and on a roll towards a huge success.
- Complementary colleagues: the copywriter and the graphic designer, the buyer and the accountant and the designer and the developer.
- Fighting boredom and loneliness, colleagues often make arrangements to organize some part-time co-working. Some days they work together, some days they don't. That's the best of both worlds.
- Mums and dads working from home can share their office with their children who are studying. They might even learn something too.
- The restless worker: the kind of person that needs a change of scene a few times a day. He or she likes to change desks every now and then. The Duo Office can be used by two of these workers, who can swap places every few hours.

Working from home can become very lonely, especially for those who crave a little feedback or just enjoy the occasional chitchat. That's why the Duo Office is an interesting alternative to the usual single layout. It doesn't have to be your partner in life who works with you every day. Why not invite a colleague over once a week? Like any good relationship, the Duo Office can offer different levels of intimacy. The most intimate Duo Office is the shared desk that means sitting next to each other. Seeing each other's desktop all the time, even when you are shopping online or checking how the football game is going, requires good mutual understanding. At the other end of the spectrum, you could have two separate desks, organized independently but still in the same room. It is easy to maintain some privacy here without getting lonely. All in all, the Duo Office is a very flexible office. It can be adapted to single working or double, depending on the specific situation or the project you are working on. Working together is without a doubt a way to double the fun, but it also requires the workers to agree on lots of things. Who gets the nicest view? Who will go for coffee? And who gets to Zoom first?

«

Do you need to see each other's computer screen very often? If so, go for the double seat, so you sit next to each other. Side by side.

»

A Duo Office will definitely determine the look and feel of a room. Do not overdecorate the rest of the space. Just add some Zen artwork to keep that inspiration flowing.

THE.DUO.OFFICE.

THE.DUO.OFFICE.

2
0
S
K
7
6

DEUTSCHE LEVANTE-LINIE HAMBURG

HOW TO MAKE THE DUO OFFICE WORK

1

— In order to make the Duo Office work: choose your co-worker wisely. Do not underestimate the social skills required to work with someone else in the same room.

2

— Decorating for two can be tricky. Don't try to please both of you by creating two totally different working spaces.

3

— Keep the basic office uniform, and try to distinguish the two workers by adding a few different and specific accessories. That way both personalities will come across.

4

— Create a logical flow in the Duo Office. Make sure you can move around in the office without bumping into cabinets, or each other.

THE. BEDROOM . OFFICE.

This might just be the most controversial chapter in this book. Almost all doctors and psychologists would advise you not to put a computer in your bedroom. It interferes with your sleeping patterns, causes stress and reminds you – even in the middle of the night – that there is work waiting to be done. So, the most important advice would be to be careful when integrating a workstation into the bedroom. On the other hand, if you are in the habit of working from your bed – which is so much worse – a desk might be a healthy improvement instead of a bad idea. It all depends on the way you work and sleep. Can your job become quite repetitive and risk making you sleepy? Then working next to a bed might not be the best idea. The same thing applies to bad sleepers who worry about work. Waking up and heading straight for your inbox is not the best way to start a new day. However a lot of people find the bedroom a very calming and relaxing space, setting the tone for a stress-reducing work environment. And of course, there are loads of workers in studios and flats all over the world, who have no choice but to integrate their desk into their bedroom.

WHO WORKS HERE?

- First and foremost, the bedroom worker has to be a good sleeper. At night, that is. People suffering from insomnia should not work in the space where they sleep, or try to sleep.
- Second requirement: the bedroom worker should also be a self-disciplined worker, not easily tempted by a quick afternoon nap.
- People who manage to get good results from working in the bedroom are often great multi-taskers. They can easily handle a phone call while sending emails and, at the same time, sketching new ideas.
- Bedroom workers don't search for great ideas in their workspace. They prefer it to be quiet and peaceful. For them, the bedroom is a sanctuary.
- People requiring a peaceful environment like this include writers, designers, psychological therapists, psychiatrists and counsellors.

«
When installing a desk in your bedroom, try to create some space between the bed and your desk. Directly rolling from your office chair onto your bed in the evenings is not a healthy way to go to sleep.

»
Go easy on the colours and decoration of your home office. Try to integrate the desk into the design of the bedroom as far as possible. It still has to look like an office in a bedroom, not a bed in the office.

KEN FOLLETT
THE PILLARS OF THE EARTH
DAN BROWN
THE DA VINCI CODE
AUEL
THE CLAN OF THE CAVE BEAR
AUEL
THE MAMMOTH HUNTERS
JEAN M AUEL
THE PLAINS OF PASSAGE

«

If available, a laptop is a great idea for a bedroom office, avoiding the constant presence of a screen in the room. The same idea goes for any kind of planner. Don't leave an open planner or a calendar hanging on the wall. Everything that can induce a panic attack must be gone by bedtime.

In an ideal layout, you create an outdoor view from your bedroom office; try to avoid looking over your bed the whole day. It may become more and more appealing as time goes by. In order to do so, make sure you have enough storage near your bedroom workstation.

THE.BEDROOM.OFFICE.

MODERN
DOG
One
Thirteen

1

— In bedrooms the lights are usually not that bright. Make sure you have a separate lighting source for your bedroom desk.

2

— In an ideal layout, you create an outdoor view from your bedroom office; try to avoid looking over your bed the whole day. It may become more and more appealing as time goes by.

HOW TO MAKE THE BEDROOM OFFICE WORK

3

— Make it very easy to shut all appliances off in the evening. You don't want to be woken by the repeating sound of emails popping up on your desktop. The computer has to be shut down completely before you can go to sleep.

RAVEL
FRANCE

THE. PANORAMIC. OFFICE.

There is nothing more inspiring than an amazing view of the mountains, the beach or the city skyline while working from home. It allows your thoughts to wander, which is often the best strategy to clear the mind and come up with solutions you never even thought about before. A panoramic view is without a doubt an enormous asset when it comes to integrating an office in your home. Especially in small studios and apartments, a nice view can give you some space to breathe, even if that space is located behind the window. Apart from the inspirational aspect, a panoramic view is also very healthy. It means daylight gets the chance to flow over your desk, which is both mentally and physically refreshing. When working it is important to keep a connection with the outdoors. To see what the weather is like, to notice people or even animals passing by, and especially to feel when the day is ending. Connecting with your surroundings offers you a chance to follow nature's rhythm, to open your laptop no earlier than dawn, and to close it again no later than dusk. Finally, seeing the outdoor world is a good motivator to go out there once in a while. To take a walk, to grab a coffee or take a dive when you are really lucky.

WHO WORKS HERE?

- The Panoramic Office is the ideal working environment for the dreamer: for the screenwriter visualizing an exciting new story, the songwriter coming up with a global hit song and also the judge contemplating his or her next decision.
- The worker with a view is someone enjoying the outdoors and needing the connection with the outdoor life, even amidst the stress of work.
- On the other hand, the panoramic worker has to be very dutiful. Thoughts can drift off really quickly. It is a gift to be able to turn those moments into useful inspirations instead of wondering about the destination of your next holiday.
- The Panoramic Office owner shouldn't be too messy. Clutter only blocks the great view.
- Whoever installs an office at a large window takes work very seriously. It is a kind of sacrifice to assign a breathtaking view to a working place. One could have chosen to install a cosy reading chair instead.

THE.PANORAMIC.OFFICE.

»
Make sure the windows are well insulated, avoiding the workstation to becoming too hot or cold and also blocking out distractive noise.

«
When there is an amazing view enhancing the room, don't go for heavy or dark office furniture. In other words: keep it light, both in colour and form.

3 00

»

Don't ever take a panoramic view for granted. Once in a while, please take your time to really look outside and consider yourself terribly lucky to be able to work in such a great environment.

»

The same goes for the desk decoration. Let the sight suck up all the attention in the room. Too many objects in front of a room can easily become a mess.

THE.PANORAMIC.OFFICE.

THE.PANORAMIC.OFFICE.

HOW TO MAKE THE PANORAMIC OFFICE WORK

1

— The most important and most obvious rule when installing a Panoramic Office is that you make sure you have a good view. Taking in the panoramic view should not require any turning or moving about.

2

— Another important detail: make sure you don't install a huge computer screen blocking a large part of the view.

3

— When you choose to go for a side view, please test whether the incoming daylight is bothering the view of your computer screen. If needed you can always provide sun screens, although it is always a pity to block an inspiring sight.

4

— Take into account that a window works both ways and that sometimes passers-by can easily look into your house. Make sure you have a good 'I am working so hard right now'-face.

VERANNEMAN
ELLIOTT ERWITT'S PARIS
CONNIE PALMEN
DE FOUTEN

THE. LIVING. OFFICE.

WHO WORKS HERE?

- People enjoying the Living Office are usually socialites, enjoying being in the centre of the action.
- Especially because of that tendency, the Living Office requires a very disciplined worker. Do not underestimate the attractive power of a television looking your way.
- The Living Office is usually not the place to sit out a full-time job. It is the home office of people with a day-time job in the outside world who return home just to finish off some extra work, or to reward themselves with some online shopping or gaming.
- People enjoying the comfort of a Living Office are for instance teachers, medical workers, people in construction and students.
- Some people just use the Living Office as an intellectual addition to their interior design. You would be surprised how many of those Living Offices are merely decorative.

What is the worst thing that can happen after a busy day at the office? It is plopping down on the sofa and then realizing you just forgot to send that crucial last email to your boss. How convenient it is then to have a small desk waiting for you right beside that sofa, providing all the comfort and devices enabling you to quickly send that email and return to your evening soap opera on TV. The Living Office, situated in the living room, is usually not a very large working station. It is hardly ever the main working station either, but the 'extra' desk in the house, installed for anyone in need of a quick (home) work fix. The Living Office is also the preferred office for those living in a tiny house or a very small apartment. When given the choice where to add an extra desk, the living room is often the first space to come up. It is also where a small office seems logical, as opposed to the bathroom or the hallway. And as parents, or suspicious spouses, might be aware: in a Living Office, everybody can see what you are doing on that laptop. For some, that would be an extra motivation to work that tiny bit harder.

The Living Office is usually not the place to sit out a full-time job. It is the home office of people with a day-time job in the outside world who return home just to finish off some extra work, or to reward themselves with some online shopping or gaming.

DOISNEAU
MARVILLE
AFRICAIN
GIACOMETTI
Van Gogh
AVEDON
Anselm Kiefer
FRANCIS PICABIA
MINIMALISME
BACON
Titien

⌄

The Living Office requires a very disciplined worker. Do not underestimate the attractive power of a television looking your way.

»

A Living Office that is not being used for eight hours a day gives you the opportunity to use flexible seating at the desk, like kitchen chairs or small stools.

1

— People enjoying the Living Office are usually socialites, enjoying being in the centre of the action.

2

— People enjoying the comfort of a Living Office are for instance teachers, medical workers, people in construction and students.

HOW TO MAKE THE LIVING OFFICE WORK

3

— Some people just use the Living Office as an intellectual addition to their interior design. You would be surprised how many of those Living Offices are merely decorative.

THE. IN/OUT OF THE BOX . OFFICE.

WHO WORKS HERE?

- The In The Box Office requires some serious out of the box thinking, so it is mainly creative people who are crazy enough to install such an office construction.
- People loving this way of working are for instance creative directors, architects, graphic designers and people in advertising.
- The in the box worker is someone who loves well-defined boundaries between work and private life. When they leave their creative box it is time to focus on family and friends.
- Privacy is crucial. The in the box worker needs private time to focus on work and therefore retreats into his or her own world.
- The In/Out of the Box Office is a full-blown home office. One does not go to the effort of installing a well-equipped studiolo just to use it just weekly. This worker enjoys working here every single day, since it often outclasses all other offices.

You don't really have a spare room to decorate as a home office? The answer is quite simple: just build one. More and more people are creating new spaces inside garages, warehouses and even living rooms that function as a home office. This so-called 'studiolo' concept is not really new. In the Italian Renaissance it originated in palazzos as a small room, often lavishly decorated, dedicated to reading, studying and writing. From there it was only a small step towards the home office. The In The Box Office is mainly a room within a room, a box if you want, setting the boundaries of your working space. In modern architecture there is definitely a tendency to think in terms of 'volumes' rather than rooms, doors and hallways. The studiolo-like concept is a great example of that volume-based thinking. But creating an extra room also offers more mental volume in your head. It is so much easier to separate work from leisure when there are actual walls defining that separation. Finally, isolating the home office delivers more creative freedom as well: it doesn't have to match anything. So please, go crazy with this one.

The first and most important requirement for this kind of workstation is space. Not a spare room, but a large garage, an atelier, a shed, a garden even. Try not to hide the box character of your home office. On the contrary, try to accentuate it. You can do that by painting the whole box in the same colour, visually separating it from the rest of the house.

Although the box is an isolated volume, please create a link with your surroundings by creating some windows or a door you can leave open. Otherwise, the In the Box Office can become quite claustrophobic.
It is important to treat this box office as a coherent unit. It doesn't have to match any style you have going on in the rest of the house, but within the box you have to be very rigorous: one style, one colour and an absolute minimum of different materials and decoration.

WECUBE
A SMILE
IN THE

HOW TO MAKE THE INOUT THEBOX OFFICE WORK

1
— Make sure all electrical requirements are present in order to install all your devices as well as lighting and heating.

2
— This is not the kind of office you install in one day. You need professional construction workers to make sure the box is stable and well isolated.

3
— Be sure to insulate your new home office as well as to include some acoustic materials. An actual empty box can be both very cold and noisy.

4
— Try not to hide the box character of your home office. On the contrary, try to accentuate it. You can do that by painting the whole box in the same colour, visually separating it from the rest of the house.

CCCP
The Stranger's Child
Alan Hollinghurst
MISSCHIEN WISTEN
Paintings
CABINET OF NATURAL CURIOSITIES
Intérieurs californiens
Intérieurs de l'Inde
LES HOMMES
WES ANDERSON
Tricia Guild
in town
ROOM
Inside Contemporary Interiors
BAZAAR STYLE
London Living

THE. TINY. OFFICE.

When it comes to home offices, the cliché is definitely true: size doesn't matter. The same goes for another cliché: less is more. Having a small or really Tiny Office doesn't make you an inferior worker. There are a lot of good reasons for installing a tiny office, the best one being not simply owning the space to set up an elaborate office. But there are others: maybe you don't want to put a desk in your beautiful living room, drawing all the attention away from your perfectly upholstered sofa. Or you might simply not need a big desk. When you require only the space to answer a few emails after dinner, it makes no sense to create an office fit for a CEO. The Tiny Office can also be a self-defence mechanism. The smaller the desk, the more limited the clutter you can spread on (and around) it. Good organization is essential on the tiny desk, as well as decoration that blends with your interior design. Typical of the Tiny Office is also the use of a design chair. People working in Tiny Offices often don't want (or need) a large ergonomic office chair but choose an elegant alternative, often matching the dining room or kitchen chairs. As you might have learned by now: the secret of a Tiny Office is blending in a very cool and elegant way – focusing more on the aesthetics than on creating a highly equipped office.

WHO WORKS HERE?

- For many home workers, the Tiny Office is often their secondary home office. While the main office is situated upstairs or in a separate room, the Tiny Office serves as a small extra for doing some late-night administrative work.
- Many jobs don't actually require a large desk. Think about the gymnastics teacher who just has to do some marking at home, the actor managing his or her agenda or the construction worker making quotes.
- Tiny Offices are often occupied by interior enthusiasts. A Tiny Office can blend in perfectly with any given interior design style and doesn't take over the aesthetics of your home. It is a subtle way of allowing work into your living area.
- Like the Zen Office, the Tiny Office requires a lot of self-discipline. Tiny means organized, so whoever is working here has to clean up after themselves.
- Beware of the downsides of a Tiny Office: if you need a lot of books and paperwork around you, then maybe this is not the ideal solution for you. The same goes for those who need several computer screens, drawing pads or audiovisual installations.

MY FAVOURITE RECIPE CLIPPINGS

«

Use your space wisely. However tiny your office is be sure to optimize the room for your desk and storage space. A floating desk is often a clever way to save some space.

⌃

Think high: when your horizontal space is limited, think vertically. Use the walls to hang shelving, a desk or storage cabinets.

THE.TINY.OFFICE.

noguchi

Keep it simple. The Tiny Office will look even tinier if you overload it. Try to keep the desk as clean as possible. Tiny and tidy.

HOW TO MAKE THE TINY OFFICE WORK

1
— In order to blend the office in, make sure to use the same style, colour and materials that are applied in the rest of your home.

2
— Don't forget to consider the corners of your space when integrating a Tiny Office. A corner offers double the wall space, so it doubles the chances of hanging shelving or cabinets.

3
— When your office is tiny, don't overdo it on the computer front. A laptop is ideal; you can just put it away in the evenings. A Tiny Office loses its charm when you put a huge screen in there.

4
— The same goes for the office chair. Go for a regular, good chair matching those in your kitchen or dining room.

THE. ZEN. OFFICE.

WHO WORKS HERE?

- The Zen Office requires a very neat personality, a trait that can often be detected in accountants, teachers and financial controllers.
- Thinking clearly without too many external stimuli can also be associated with creative people like poets or songwriters, people who want to begin every single project with a clean slate.
- The Zen worker has enormous amounts of discipline, making sure nothing stands in the way of the peaceful layout that characterizes this kind of office.
- Of course yoga trainers, mindfulness coaches and therapists of all kinds will use their Zen Office as a signature style.
- The Zen Office can also be used as a compensation for a very boisterous and noisy day-to-day life. We can imagine a nursery teacher, a shop assistant or a busy HR manager using the Zen Office merely as a place to cool down in the evening.

Some get inspired by books, others by nice family photographs or an impressive view, and then there are the true aesthetes who draw their inspiration from absolutely nothing. Good ideas come while they are staring blankly into the empty space around them. Do not confuse the Zen Office with the popular clean desk policy applied in many big companies. The Zen Office is not just about leaving your desk totally empty at the end of the day; it is a state of mind. A very peaceful state of mind obviously. Zen adepts consider their desk as a kind of sanctuary, a shrine where they can think clearly about life's big questions. But, in order to achieve that, the Zen Office requires a huge amount of discipline. Every little object within eyesight is a burden for the peace of mind that makes this kind of office unique. In order to keep the overall ambiance of the Zen Office warm and inviting, colours are soft and materials very natural. Even at this end of the clutter spectrum, one can go too far. You don't want to get the impression that you are writing on a desk that was just put in yesterday and is not finished yet. Nor feel you are calling colleagues from a nuclear bunker. It is staying on the right side of the thin line between relaxing and peaceful on the one hand, and sterile and cold on the other, that makes the Zen Office quite a challenge to create.

There is no point in creating a Zen Office in an eclectic and maximalist interior. It would just fade away. Make sure the Zen Office is aligned with your overall interior style.

THE.ZEN.OFFICE.

A Zen Office doesn't have to be totally free of any kind of decoration. But keep it very simple. Pick one vase, one lamp or one piece of art, to steal the show.

Make sure you have nice textures in your office. A wooden chair, a soft carpet... Texture gives any interior design warmth and cosiness and that's exactly what it is hard to achieve in a Zen Office.

THE.ZEN.OFFICE.

THE.ZEN.OFFICE.

HOW TO MAKE THE ZEN OFFICE WORK

1
— The first thing you have to determine is whether you have the skills to maintain a Zen Office. Are you the kind of person to clean up after every single task?

2
— Make sure you have plenty of storage space. An empty desk means you need a cupboard for paperwork and accessories.

3
— Choose neutral colours to create a soothing environment. The Zen factor will quickly disappear if you paint your desk in bright orange.

4
— Be aware that white isn't the best Zen colour in the world. Go for off-white or beige instead;they evoke a more comforting feeling than bright white walls.

COLORS
Extraordinary Records
Außergewöhnliche Schallplatten
Disques extraordinaires
TASCHEN
Extraordinary Records

CREDITS.

Concept & texts
An Bogaert

Editing
Blue Lines

Book Design
Tina Smedts – De Poedelfabriek

Sign up for our newsletter with news about new and forthcoming publications on art, interior design, food & travel, photography and fashion as well as exclusive offers and events.

If you have any questions or comments about the material in this book, please do not hesitate to contact our editorial team: art@lannoo.com

D/2021/45/268– NUR 450/454
ISBN: 9789401478335
www.lannoo.com

COVER.
© Jan Verlinde / interior design by Thomas Serruys

TABLE.OF.CONTENTS.
p.6 Image by Montana Furniture

THE.LIBRARY.OFFICE.
p.8 © Jan Verlinde
p.10–11, p.19 © Unsplash
p.12, p.16–17 Image by VITRA
p.13 © Jan Verlinde
p.14–15 Photofoyer / Architect Elena Cerizza / stylist Laura Mauceri / photo Cristina Galliena Bohman
p.18 Photofoyer / Unduo Architekture / Stylist Laura Mauceri / photo Cristina Galliena Bohman
p.21 © Mr.Frank

THE.HEALTHY.OFFICE.
p.22, p.24–25, p.28 © HEIMHOLZ by Siehr, founder and designer Axel Siehr, Patrick Siehr, www.heimholz.shop
p.26 © Henrietta Williams for Studio Ben Allen
p.27, p.29, p.31 © Unsplash

THE.GALLERY.OFFICE.
p.32, p.34, p.39 Photofoyer / Photo Montse Garriga Grau
p.35 Photofoyer / Architect Julie de Halleaux / photo Mireille Roobaert
p.36, p.38, p.41 © Unsplash
p.37 Photofoyer / Designer Chris Glass House / photo Daniel Schaefer
p.40 Photofoyer / Design by Quintana Partners / Photo Daniel Schaefer
p.42 © Luc Roymans Photography / Nelson De Coninck @nelplant
p.43 Photofoyer/ photo Fabrizio Cicconi / Styling Francesca Davoli
p.45 @ Kaatje Verschoren, www.photograffiti-kaatje.com / interior design by Atelier Piraat

THE.INVENTIVE.OFFICE.
p.46 Gran Via apartment in Barcelona by architects Anna & Eugeni Bach, 2015 © Eugeni Bach
p.48–49: House of Rolf designed by Studio Rolf.fr in cooperation with Niek Wagemans, © Christel Derksen & Rolf Bruggink, www.rolf.fr, www.fabriekvanniek.nl
p.50–51: © Jan Verlinde / design by Lens°ass Architects
p.52 @ Kaatje Verschoren, www.photograffiti-kaatje.com / design Bearandbunny Amsterdam
p.53 balKonzept by Michael Hilgers for Rephorm,

www.michaelhilgers.de, www.rephorm.de
p.55 © Unsplash

THE.GLAMOUR.OFFICE.
p.56, p.58, p.62, p.63 Photofoyer / Photo Montse Garriga Grau
p.59 @ Kaatje Verschoren, www.photograffiti-kaatje.com / design by VELOR architecten
p.60-61 Photofoyer / photo Monika Lewandowska

p.64 Photofoyer / photo Richard Powers

p.65, p.67 © BRABBU Design Forces

THE.NATURAL.OFFICE.
p.68 Photofoyer / Photo Martyna Rudnicka
p.70, p.75 Photofoyer / photo Fabienne Delafraye
p.71, p.79 © Unsplash
p.72-73: © Jan Verlinde
p.74 Image by VITRA
p.76-77 © Victor Roussel for PETITE-FRITURE, January 2021

THE.HIDDEN.OFFICE.
p.80 PIRANDELLO desk, design Jasper Morrison, production Glasitalia, www.glasitalia.com
p.82 © Jan Verlinde / Design by Tenarchitects
p.83, p.87 Image by Ligne Roset
p.84 © Luc Roymans Photography / design by Van Staeyen interieurarchitecten, www.vanstaeyen.be
p.85 © Megan Taylor / design by 2LG Studio

THE.PLAYFUL.OFFICE.
p.88 Photofoyer / photo Montse Garriga Grau
p.90 Image by Montana Furniture
p.91, p.95, p.97, p.103 © Unsplash
p.92 @ Kaatje Verschoren, www.photograffiti-kaatje.com
p.93 © Photofoyer / Home of Thierry Gilier / photo Rei Moon
p.94 © Luc Roymans Photography / design by Van Staeyen interieurarchitecten, www.vanstaeyen.be
p.96 Photofoyer / photo Martyna Rudnicka
p.98 Photofoyer / homeowner Gilles Dewavrin / Photo Mireille Roobaert
p.99 Photofoyer / photo Celestyna Krol
p.100 © Photofoyer / Photo Leo Zappert
p.101 © Jan Verlinde / design by Studio Suchalike

THE.MESSY.OFFICE.
p.104 Unsplash
p.106, p.107 Photofoyer / photo Cristina Galliena Bohman
p.108, p.109 Photofoyer / photo Richard Powers
p.110-111 Photofoyer / Elena Salmistraro Studio / Photo Filippo Bamberghi
p.113 © Jan Verlinde

THE.VINTAGE.OFFICE.
p.114 © Jan Verlinde
p.116 Image by Ligne Roset
p.117 © Jan Verlinde / Frank Pay showroom144.be
p.118, p.119, p.122, p.123 © Unsplash
p.120 @ Kaatje Verschoren, www.photograffiti-kaatje.com / owned and designed by Shirley Muijrers and Olaf Arkauer from SUITE702 luxury bedding
p.121 © Jan Verlinde / design by Michel Penneman
p.125 © Jan Verlinde / interior design by Thomas Serruys

THE.KITCHEN.OFFICE.
p.126 © Tess Kelly Photography / Alfred House by Austin Maynard Architects
p.128 © Mr.Frank
p.129 © Fabio Marullo for Living Inside
p.130 © Tess Kelly Photography / Alfred House by Austin Maynard Architects
p.131, p.135 © Unsplash
p.132 © Tess Kelly Photography / Long House by Clare Cousins Architects
p.133 Photofoyer / Photo Marcin Grabowiecki

THE.DUO.OFFICE.
p.136 © Unsplash
p.138 Photofoyer / Designer George Nakashima / photo Manolo Yllera
p.139 Image by Ethnicraft
p.140 Image by ferm LIVING
p.141 Photofoyer / Photo Jordi Miralles
p.142 © Jan Verlinde
p.143 © Luc Roymans Photography/ design @ C52_Antwerp
p.145 © Jan Verlinde

THE.BEDROOM.OFFICE.
p.146 Photofoyer / Interior design by AVC interiors / Photo Anna Stathaki
p.148, p.149 Photofoyer / photo Leo Zappert
p.150 © Mr.Frank
p.151 © Unsplash
p.152, p.153 Photofoyer / photo Pablo Veiga
p.154-155 © Unsplash
p.157 Photofoyer / Photo Manolo Yllera

THE.PANORAMIC.OFFICE.
p.158 © Photofoyer / Home of Isabelle Mallevays, co-founder of The Invisible Collection / Photo Bénèdicte Drummond
p.160 Image by Ligne Roset
p.161 © BRABBU Design Forces
p.162 © Jan Verlinde
p.163 Photofoyer / Sophie Cauvin House / Photo Mireille Roobaert
p.164 © Unsplash
p.165, p.169 Image by Wewood - Portuguese Joinery
p.166 Photofoyer / Photo Mige G/Alicja T.
p.167 © Jan Verlinde
p.168 Image by VITRA
p.171 © Anders Schonnemann for &Tradition

THE.LIVING.OFFICE.
p.172 © Jan Verlinde / Design by AE Studio
p.174-175 © Jan Verlinde
p.176, p.177, p.179 © Unsplash
p.178 Photofoyer / photo Richard Powers
p.180 © Jan Verlinde / design by BCINT
p.181 © Luc Roymans Photography / Design, production & realisation by Atelierpiraat
p.182-183 Photofoyer / photo Catherine Gailloud
p.185 © Jan Verlinde

THE.IN/OUT.OF.THE.BOX.OFFICE.
p.186, p.195 © Luc Roymans Photography / design by Van Staeyen interieurarchitecten, www.vanstaeyen.be
p.188-189 © Luc Roymans Photography / design by STUDIOLO architectuur
p.190-191 © Tim Van De Velde Photography / design by Nathalie Wolberg Architect
p.192-193 wecube - www.wecube.be

THE.TINY.OFFICE.
p.196 © Jan Verlinde / design by Kim Verbist Interiors
p.198, p.199, p.205 © Unsplash
p.200 Image by ferm LIVING
p.201 Image by Quick-Step
p.202 Photofoyer / homeowner Gilles Dewavrin / Photo Mireille Roobaert
p.203 Image by HAY
p.204 Image by VITRA
p.207 © Jan Verlinde

THE.ZEN.OFFICE.
p.208 © Jan Verlinde / design by Arjaan De Feyter Interior Architects
p.210-211 © Cafeine for BULO, H2O Table designed with Claire Bataille and Paul Ibens, SL58 office chair inspired by Léon Stynen
p.212 Image by Ethnicraft
p.213 Image by Studio HENK
p.214-215, p.216, p.217, p.219, p.224 © Unsplash
p.218 © Emeco
p.221 Image by Ligne Roset

Visual Storytelling